Adam's Story

Adam's Story

◆

The miracle you pray for isn't always the miracle you get...

Allison Carver Harrison

iUniverse, Inc.
New York Lincoln Shanghai

Adam's Story
The miracle you pray for isn't always the miracle you get…

All Rights Reserved © 2004 by Allison Carver Harrison

No part of this book may be reproduced or transmitted in any form or by any means, graphic, electronic, or mechanical, including photocopying, recording, taping, or by any information storage retrieval system, without the written permission of the publisher.

iUniverse, Inc.

For information address:
iUniverse, Inc.
2021 Pine Lake Road, Suite 100
Lincoln, NE 68512
www.iuniverse.com

ISBN: 0-595-31313-2

Printed in the United States of America

I dedicate this story to the memory of my precious friend, Mary Jane, who is now in Heaven with my darling son. She was always "on my side" even when I didn't deserve her to be. She taught me Christianity by demonstrating what it means to be a servant and to love unconditionally.

Foreword

I got acquainted with Allison in the spring on 1978 when I was falling in love with her younger brother. Nick and I were students at UW-Madison and frequently visited Allison and her family in Milwaukee. Her newly embraced evangelical Christian faith was straightforward, enthusiastic and vocal. Her children were the focus of her attention and life and their house was like that of the comic "Family Circus"—it was fun! Six people and many animals in a small house, lots of music, sports, food and laughter, many visitors.

God could have allowed the tranquility to go on, but He did not. Allison was about to face what every mother has had nightmares about: the loss of her small child. Nick and I were there at Adam's two-year-old birthday party. Little did we know what lay ahead for Adam and the whole family, especially for Allison. The next ten years were full of shocking experiences, raised hopes, dashed hopes, broken relationships and healed hearts. As a sister-in-law, I have watched Allison from a close vantage point. There were times when I felt so close to her that all I could do was cry. There were times when I was so frustrated with her that I didn't want to be with her. What I came to understand is that Allison had her own timetable of grief and recovery, known and understood only by God.

In recent years, we've become close friends on a whole new level. Two years ago, she confided in me that she wanted to write a book about Adam. She wanted to leave a legacy of Adam's life and her experiences to her other children. I thought it was a fantastic idea and I am so proud of her for following through on the writing.

This is not a book for people who think that once one becomes a Christian, everything in life falls into place. This is a book for people who have come to see that life is messy and sometimes very bleak. But this is a book of hope in the midst of pain, because as Allison has learned, our Lord Jesus Christ is with his children no matter what. I can't paraphrase the words of the Lord better than the hymn writer has done it:

> "When through the deep waters I cause thee to go
> The rivers of sorrow will not overflow.
> For I will be with thee, thy troubles to bless
> And sanctify to thee thy deepest distress."
> (Stanza 3 of "How Firm A Foundation" from Rioppon's *Selection of Hymns*, 1787)
>
> Ruth Thompson Carver

Prologue

I have a story to share with you. It is a story of highs and lows, good and bad, happy and sad, but mostly about a powerful and almighty God who gives us a reason to hope and a desire to live. It is about my youngest son, Adam, who is now in Heaven with his heavenly father. I believe that he has so many jewels in his crown that his head slants a little to one side! I think that is how I will recognize him one day when I finally get to see him again.

I have written Adam's story, mostly for my living children, so they may read it and cherish the memories. So that they also will be reminded of the deep and abiding love our Lord has for each of us.

I think, too, of the other families who are touched by tragedy and loss, the heartache that follows and God's love in the midst of it all. Without the knowledge that God is in control, I could not have survived my loss of Adam. God surely must love me-love us-a lot!

Adam Mark was my third child, born on August 12, 1976. Waiting to eagerly meet him were three siblings. Timothy, my stepson, was nine, Rachel was four and Benjamin was almost two. I was 26 and had my hands full! Earlier in the day on which Adam was born, I took Rachel to see the movie, "Tom Sawyer" while Ben went to play with his cousin. After the movie, we picked up Ben and went to my mom's house for a leisurely dinner on the patio that she shared with her brother, my Uncle Dan. It was a gorgeous summer evening that changed abruptly when I stood up and "spilled my tea", as Rachel later told everyone. I was in labor! So back to my cousin's house Rachel and Ben went while Mom and I sped off to the hospital. My husband, Gary, promptly left work and followed.

Adam arrived soon after, our doctor exclaiming that he had never delivered such a long baby, 23 ½ inches long and 8lbs. 12 oz! From the first second I layed eyes on him and kissed his precious forehead, I adored that little boy. In years to come I would often question, "did I love him too much? Is that why God took him?" But now I'm getting ahead of the story...

That winter was a special time of closeness for our family, particularly for the kids. We didn't have a second car and with three small children, we spent a lot of time at home. Adam grew quickly and by the time he was fifteen months old, he and Ben were very close in size and soon were daily mistaken for twins. The boys got along perfectly and Rachel loved mothering them both. Of course they all adored their big brother, Tim, who came to live with us that year.

We were a busy family. I remember one time on a Sunday morning arriving at Elmbrook Church with all of my children in tow. I bumped into Jill Briscoe, our pastor's wife outside. She said. "My goodness, Allison, are they all yours?" I loved being a mother, teaching Child Evangelism five day clubs in the summer, having neighborhood Bible clubs in our home, teaching children's church on Sunday mornings. We had close Christian friends, our children were the lights of our lives and all of them were bright, beautiful and healthy. What more could we ask for?

The next winter my mom, my closest friend, moved to California to join Campus Crusade for Christ to work in the women's prisons there. My sister often kidded her that we had given her lots of practice for prison ministry while we were growing up! Mom's example of following God's call really taught me the lesson of putting God first. I treasure that lesson. That Easter our family drove out to southern California to visit my mom. On the third night of our visit, Rachel, always the little nurturer, called me into the bedroom. Ben wanted to ask Jesus into his heart NOW! What could I do but kneel and pray with that little three year old right then and there! Halleluia! Another prayer answered.

By the summer of 1978, Adam was growing strong, both spiritually as well as physically. A joy to all who met him, Adam talked early and often about spiritual things. In the morning he would run into the kitchen and squeal "a morning, Mama", climb onto the table and sing, "Stand up a Jesus!" He knew and understood about God in a deep way at only 21 months. He would have conversations with his dad about the Creator. "Who made trees Dad? God? Who made animals, Dad? God? Who made cars, Dad? Man?" I adored all of my children equally, but Adam was my baby. He didn't want to be though, he wanted to run, jump, swim, ride bikes, draw pictures, everything that his siblings did. I held him close and prayed for him and the other children. I prayed for their continued good health, for their future spouses, for the big events in their lives, but mostly that they would choose to follow God all of the days of their lives.

That August our dear friends from Texas, Bill and Sarah Stewart and their five children, came to visit us for Rachel and Adam's birthdays. We had a huge outdoor party with lots of family and friends. Adam was out of diapers and my funniest memory is of him "relieving himself" on the front lawn. My husband happened to videotape the incident. I didn't know at the time how grateful I would be to have this fun and funny day recorded. The many children swam in our little pool in the back yard as we adults sat under the shade of our beautiful old maple tree, enjoying God's beauty and thanking Him for the gifts being lent to us in the back yard.

Ben started preschool in August, and with Rachel and Tim also in school, I had Adam to myself for a short time every day. I enjoyed those times immensely. He was an easy child to love. His was a consistent disposition. He rarely needed scolding. I could reason with him and he would obey. Again at times I would ask God if I loved Adam too much. I was reminded of when I was a young teen and had just acknowledged that I needed a Savior. My mom became friends with a Baptist pastor and his family. One day, the pastor's wife took me aside and told me the story of having to give up roller skating as a family because they loved it too much. This sentence always haunted me and never rang true. It did sit in my deep subconscious, though, especially as I thought about my deep love for Adam. About that time Adam started showing symptoms of illness. He was more tired than usual, had lost his appetite, and had a "whistle" in his breathing. I took him to the doctor four times in September. One doctor diagnosed pneumonia and hospitalized Adam for a week. Another treated him for allergies, flu, virus, but Adam continued to fail.

I am a woman of action, always doing things ahead of time when possible. I anticipate a crisis may happen at the last minute so I like to be prepared. That September I made all of the children matching clown outfits for Halloween and took their picture on the front porch of our cape cod to use in our annual Christmas card. I was so grateful, even elated, in months ahead that I had done that. My three children looked darling sitting on the steps surrounded by pumpkins. Did I "sense" imminent loss or tragedy? I am not sure, but I do know that I was prompted to take that picture when I did. Do I usually take Christmas pictures in September? Not before or after.

October came and Adam was still not well. He had lost five pounds and was becoming quite weak. Finally on October 10, I told my husband that after I drove the children to school, I was taking Adam directly to the doctor. I would insist that he discover what was causing my son to fail right before my very eyes. I stopped at my best friend, Diane's, house and she assured me that I was doing the right thing.

We arrived at the office at 9am and Adam's doctor saw us immediately. He took one look at Adam and one listen to his chest and his face said it all. He told me that Adam's right lung had collapsed. He would give him a shot of adrenalin to re-inflate it and so he could figure out the cause. Adam's lung did not re-inflate as planned and we were sent directly to the hospital where Adam would be admitted. I was a wreck. I pleaded with God to make him well. I bargained. I promised. I prayed, "Please, God, don't take my Adam from me. I can't live without him. I don't want to live without him. Please, God, please…" I called my husband at work and my mom in California. She would inform her prayer chain. I called our church. I called our two close friends who are doctors. Everyone was confident that Adam would be fine.

In the morning the pulmonary doctor would perform a bronchoscopy to seek the foreign object in his lung that was causing the distress. X-rays had showed nothing, just fluid filling his lung. I continued to think about the many questions the doctors had asked me about the possible causes of his illness, and it was then that I remember the peanuts we had at the birthday party in August. I was taking them away from Adam, but he kept going back to eat more. The doctors asked me if he had choked or possibly inhaled a peanut. I could not recall. A peanut would not show up on an X-ray, but would cause infection in the lung as it deteriorated. If it were a peanut, the bronchoscope would bring it up. Adam would be fine—a day or two of swelling in his throat and he would go home on Saturday, October 14. I questioned the doctor, "what were the chances of something going wrong?" I was told one in a million, but was still uneasy. I prayed. I asked others to pray. And I confess that I worried. Each time I would cast all my cares on Him who loved us, I would take those cares back again. So much to learn, so much that my heavenly Father wanted to teach me, so much that He wanted to do, if only I would let him. The procedure was performed early the next morning. It had indeed been a peanut in his lung for six weeks. The peanut had rotted and when touched with the bronchoscope it fell into many pieces. Each piece had to be taken up his esophagus and out his mouth. The instrument was too large, causing far more swelling than anyone anticipated. The distress began. When we finally had the opportunity to see our darling boy, he was having great difficulty breathing. His lips and fingertips were blue. I reached into the oxygen tent to hug him, to tell him that he would be all right and that he would go home to his brothers and sister tomorrow, he would be perfect again. He slowly turned to me with desperation in his eyes and whispered "Pray, Mama." I bowed my head as I held his tiny hand in mine and prayed with him. I asked for healing, peace and comfort for my dying child. I sang "Jesus Loves Me" to him as the nurses pushed me aside and whisked my Adam away to intensive care. Gary was at Awana with the children that night. I finally reached him at his mom's house and I begged him to come right away. I called my mom in California and said, "Mom, Adam is dying." She said that she would be there tomorrow and she would be praying. I thanked her because I couldn't pray. I was empty inside and I had intense pain in my heart. I felt as if I was dying as well.

Friday, October 13, Adam was worse not better. Now on a ventilator he struggled with every breath. He told me that he wanted to go potty but when he tried to sit up, he didn't have the energy. I cried when the nurse came in to put a diaper on him. I saw Adam slipping away from me and I was helpless. I was assured that he would not be forced to fight for breath much longer. He would receive a trache and be able to begin healing. Because he was in ICU, we could only see Adam for ten minutes every hour. How incredibly difficult that was for a mom and dad! We talked to Adam, prayed with him, reminded him that Tim, Rachel and Ben missed and loved him.

Meanwhile the ICU waiting room was filling with family and friends. Every chair was taken and others were standing. Our pastor, Stuart Briscoe, was there and many of the deacons and their wives. They prayed over Adam, we prayed in small groups in the waiting room, our entire church was praying.

Mom would arrive soon. My Uncle Dan was picking her up at the airport and they would come directly to the hospital…

By late afternoon, Adam's little chest was sucking in for air. I pleaded with the doctors to do something-please help my little boy, the apple of my eye. "God, where are you?" I saw some movement in Adam's body that I didn't understand. Then the respiratory therapist whisked us out of Adam's room. I learned later that Adam had suffered the first of hundreds of seizures he would have. "Code blue, Code blue!" I collapsed into my husband's arms screaming, knowing in my mother's heart that the code was for my Adam. Code blue meant that he had stopped breathing. I wasn't allowed to go to Adam, I couldn't stop screaming and I couldn't pray. "What was happening? Was my baby boy alive or dead? Were the doctors finally helping him to breathe or was it too late?"

We waited frozen in time. "How long had it been? When would they come get us? Could I bear to hear what they would have to tell us?" 45 minutes later our pediatrician appeared. Adam had indeed stopped breathing for 23–25 minutes. He was in a deep coma and on a respirator. Everyone around us started to pray once again. "Did we want to see him?" Of course we wanted to see him!

As we were led into Adam's room, I was not prepared for what I would see. There were tubes everywhere. Because of the lack of oxygen to his brain for such a lengthy time, his brain was beginning to swell. His little eyes were closed but protruding from the pressure behind them. He was so very still and so very helpless. I yearned to touch him but couldn't. I wanted to talk to him but was afraid. "What had happened? What went wrong? How could this happen in the ICU with doctors present?"

After our allotted ten minutes, we were literally led back to the waiting room, which would become our home for the next thirty days. The nuns at the hospital gave up their private bath and bedroom for us, people started coming with food and prayer. I sat there stunned and numb.

Mom and Uncle Dan arrived at about nine pm. Mom hadn't seen Adam in about five months. I needed her so badly; she was always strong for me when I couldn't be. After a short stay at the hospital, she went home to be with the other children. What a blessing!

Saturday morning we met with a group of doctors. They didn't have an explanation for what had happened to Adam. They could only say that they had done all that they could and that he had stopped breathing anyway. We went back to Adam's room mindful that God was indeed in control of everything and has a plan for each of us. We would trust Him with Adam. After all, Adam did belong to Him. God had just lent him to us for as long as He had intended.

My husband went home on Sunday to spend time with the children and to tell them about their brother. One of our pastors went with Gary. Our friends, John and Diane Schmidtke met Gary and Joe at our house. They needed to prepare the children. The doctors expected Adam to die within a week. We were advised to take him off the respirator. What a lot to swallow! Rachel, Ben, and Tim cried and pleaded with their dad to be able to visit their brother. Joe also suggested we get rid of all of our pictures of Adam, especially the ones we had on display. I complied. Good grief! How could I have done that? What had he been thinking? Why did I listen to him? I now have very few pictures of my son as I knew him. The children weren't as devastated as one would expect. We were a family of prayer and we trusted in God. The children truly believed Adam would be well and would come home no matter what the doctors said.

While Gary went home, I stayed and talked to Adam constantly but was afraid I would hurt him if I touched him. Not that I believed I would hurt him physically. Instead, I was struggling with thoughts that I brought this on Adam, that I was being punished for something I had done earlier in my life. I felt that if I distanced myself from Adam, God could work in his life. Adam was getting stiff by the fourth day: his little arms were bent and rigid, his hands were in tight fists. He had a food tube in his nose leading down to his stomach. He had IV's for fluids and was receiving anti-seizure medication. He was given antibiotics when he began to run a low-grade fever. Adam's toes were pointed and very cold. I wanted to be like Gary who held him all day long, taking, singing all of Adam's favorites, and praying. I just couldn't. As week two began dear friends began to relieve us so that we could go home for short breaks. On one of those visits, Gary pulled into the driveway and ran over our dog. I started screaming uncontrollably and picked up our Corning coffeepot and threw it right through our large kitchen window! The tension was mounting and I was suffocating. Bless my dear mom who continued to stay with us and help with our children and her child, Allison, who wasn't doing very well either!

One of our dear friends, John Matthews, started coming to the hospital most evenings, sometimes staying all night so that either or both Gary and I could go home. At home there was no normalcy as we fully expected to receive a phone call at any time that Adam had died. John's presence was a life saver for us. On one of John's visits when just he, Gary and Uncle Dan were there, Adam stopped breathing. He had been doing this on and off since being weaned off of the respirator. Gary continued to hold Adam and paged the nurse. As the nurse and doctor timed his cessation of breath, my uncle, John, and Gary started to pray. They prayed for Adam's short life, offered praise for Heaven, a far better place than earth, and gave thanks that God was in control. The minutes ticked by and as Adam started to turn blue, the doctors declared that he had indeed passed away. It had been almost a half an hour. Just then Adam made a huge gulp and started to breathe again! That was the last of his breathing episodes. I remained unable to hold or touch Adam. I was reading everything I could get my hands on concerning brain damage so I knew what I should be doing. I could do the talking and play music but just not touch him.

Halloween came and the kids wore their costumes I had made them in September. Gary took them trick or treating while I stayed at the hospital. In a few weeks, on November 13, we'd celebrate Ben's birthday, just one month to the day that our Adam first died. We didn't have any idea what would happen in the weeks to come. I felt so helpless and out of control.

Ben and I started spending days at the hospital while Rachel and Tim were in school. Gary would drive the ten miles to the hospital after work and stay all night. Ben and I would go home when Gary got to the hospital. We had many dear friends picking up the other kids after school until I got home. On one of Gary's ten-mile treks to the hospital, he swerved to miss a table in the highway and hit the center medium. He arrived at the hospital in an ambulance, having sustained a concussion. That night I cared for two patients!

Elmbrook Church, our home church, was wonderful to us, especially during that first month. Every night someone in the congregation provided a meal. Every person was sad and touched by Adam's brain injury, so when they would arrive with the meal, they would usually shed a few tears and bring lots of hugs as well. The love in our church was definitely prompted by the Holy Spirit. One day while my mother and I were in the front of the house watching the children, Lynn Matrise, a good friend whose children were the ages of mine, brought a meal. We hugged and I thanked her for her prayers and the food. She said it was her specialty, lasagna. Mom looked at me and we burst out laughing. Poor Lynn had no idea that we had received lasagna every night for two weeks! I'm sure it was the first time I had laughed in weeks and it felt great!

Week three I picked up the pictures I had taken of Tim, Rachel, Ben, and Adam in September on our front porch. I looked at them in amazement. Adam looked so thin and the areas around his eyes so hollow. Why hadn't I noticed how sick he looked? Why had I waited until October 10th to take him to our pediatrician? So much had happened to our family since that picture. Life would never be the same again for any of us. All I could do was keep reminding myself that God uses "everything for good to those who love the Lord and are the called according to His purpose." I also reminded God that He promised not to give us more than we could handle. It seemed He had forgotten, because I certainly could not handle this!

Meanwhile I began to plan Ben's 4th birthday party. I didn't want the other children to get ignored on their special day so I proceeded to plan a party with all of Ben's little buddies. Ben kept reminding me that all he wanted for his birthday was for Adam to get better!

On the first Sunday in November, God moved in my life to address one of my deepest fears. I decided it was time to go back to church again. We had avoided the crowds because having so many people wanted to talk to us was emotionally draining. Mom and I went while Gary stayed at the hospital. The other children were so excited to be going back to Sunday school. We sat in the back row so as not to be conspicuous. About halfway through Stuart's sermon a startling occurrence took place. I heard God's voice so clearly that I was surprised that Mom hadn't heard it as well. He said, "Allison, Adam isn't going to die. Get up out of your seat and go to the hospital. You need to learn how to take care of him. He is coming home this week!" I got up and asked Mom to care for the kids as I was leaving. I drove straight to the hospital and walked into Adam's room. There were no feelings of nausea or the need to run into the bathroom. I sat down in the chair and asked Gary to hand Adam to me as I needed to learn how to care for him because he wasn't going to die! Speechless, Gary handed him to me and said I was right. The hospital was discharging Adam on Wednesday. I needed to learn how to feed Adam with the feeding tube, do his range of motion exercises to help to give him some movement and one million other things! I had not touched or held my little boy in almost one month. I was overwhelmed but also excited. God had spoken to me! He would equip me to do this! He really was in control!

Adam was discharged from the hospital one day before Ben's birthday. All that the children cared about was that their brother was coming home. It didn't matter to them that he was in diapers again, that he was blind, that he was so stiff he couldn't even move his head from side to side, that all he could do was cry (which he did most of the time), that he couldn't even swallow-just that he was home again! When Ben blew the candles out on his cake his wish was that Adam would get better. That was each of the children's birthday wishes for the next six years.

The change of the seasons helped bring normalcy to our lives. The leaves on our beautiful maple trees fell and Ben and Rachel played in them. One day they had formed "rooms" with the leaves and began arguing. When I intervened, Ben spoke up, "Rachel is in my coma and *I* want to be in it!" I didn't understand until he explained that he had a coma like Adam's. He thought that when we spoke of Adam being in a coma, we were referring to his bed!

One of the books I had read during this time was written by Donna Nason about her daughter, Tara. Tara had suffered a brain injury similar to Adam's. After I finished her book, I called her in California. She was very gracious and helpful. She gave me a list of suggestions which I took note of and thanked her for her time. Her husband worked for Dr Robert Schuller and I had seen Donna and Tara on the Hour of Power. God had worked wonders in Tara. Was His plan to use the same process with Adam to bring about his healing? I was willing to try anything. She suggested I try different tastes on Adam's tongue-whipped cream, popsicles, and sugar. She also suggested stimulating him with strong scents, tactile fabrics, and varied sounds. He did seem to like the foods, didn't seem to like the feeling of textures on his skin, and was easily frightened by unfamiliar sounds. I concentrated on the food. By December I could feed Adam a meal or two a day by mouth but it took at least an hour a meal! He choked a lot but I persisted. He eventually learned to swallow, but not to chew, so every bite was tiny and nothing was hard.

The second week in December Adam developed a rash so off to the doctor we went. He was still in a coma and I really couldn't even bend him so dressing him in winter clothes was very difficult. I had to make his clothes so that it was easier to put on and take off. The first question the doctor asked was where his food tube was. It was usually taped to the side of his nose when not in use. I explained that I had taken it out and was teaching Adam to eat. The doctor literally grabbed him out of my arms to weigh him and was shocked to see that he had actually gained weight! He pointed out that this was pointless as Adam was just going to get sick and die so just make him comfortable on the couch. I vowed I would never do that and I would limit my doctor visits from then on.

That year, the Christmas program for Elmbrook Church's Ladies Christmas program was live on television. Jill Briscoe asked me if I would be willing to share on the program what I was thankful for that Christmas. That was easy! I was eager to do that. I wanted to tell people that even though my youngest son would be spending Christmas in a coma that year, we knew that God was in control and truly "all things do work together for good." Later when we had Adam dedicated in church, that would be the verse we chose for him.

We came home one day the week before Christmas and our wonderful friends Dave and Claudia Anderson had come over and put up a tree for us. What a neat present! Gifts started to arrive-cases of diapers for Adam, cases of Ensure, and clothes for Tim, Rachel, and Ben. My new friend, Mary Jane, gave us a camera so we could start recording Adam's progress.

Our holiday season was wonderful. We carried Adam to all of the festivities. I was so sure he perked up whenever we sang his favorite song, "Stand up for Jesus." We invited all of our friends and their children to our neighborhood to go caroling. Adam was always included. The men usually took turns carrying him. We settled into our new life but not for long…

I called Donna Nason again after the holidays were over. I asked her about the "Institutes for the Achievement of Human Potential" in Philadelphia. She attributed a lot of Tara's healing to the rigid program of patterning through the Institutes. I was willing to give it a try. Gary wasn't quite as enthusiastic as the extra time, money, and care Adam demanded was already taking its toll on our family time, but he agreed after some discussion. I wrote to the Institutes and Adam was put on a waiting list of one and a half to two years!

Finally the call came-one year later! Ben was five, Rachel seven, and Tim was eleven. The IAHP would see Adam and evaluate him. We would also be closely scrutinized. The IAHP only wanted 100 % committed parents, willing to work with their child every waking hour of every day, seven days a week, 365 days a year-no exception. One rule broken and we were out of the program.

The IAHP was located in Philadelphia, Pa and run by a gentleman named Glen Doman. It was a highly controversial program of patterning. Four people moving Adam's limbs for him in a crawling motion. Their theory was that the undamaged brain cells could be patterned to take over for the dead brain cells and be taught by intensity, frequency and duration. The Institutes philosophy became our philosophy. When we weren't patterning Adam's brain to crawl, we had him on an incline plane trying to coax him down it. Unfortunately the only movement we saw was when Adam cried and slid a little. Everything we did had to be recorded. Every week we had to report in to our coach in Philadelphia by phone. A wonderful woman from our church, whom we had never met before, took it upon herself to schedule our volunteers. Margie found subs when someone was unable to make their time slot. Of course Margie was one of them! Fifty two volunteers came in and out of our home every week from 8 am until 6pm. We showed Adam's blind eyes pictures-100's a day. Rachel was especially good at that. We shined eight 100 watt light bulbs on and off, on and off into those same blind eyes for a total of two hours a day. Tim was a great help with that tedious job. Ben pushed Adam in his wheelchair in the driveway. One of the Institute's requirements was that either I or his dad had to be involved at all times. Whether we were hanging him upside down to increase blood circulation into his brain, putting a mask over his mouth and nose to teach him to breath deeper, telling him about sounds, textures, smells, or the patterning, one of us was there. Gary worked, we had four young children, but I spent most of every day in the basement with Adam recording "patterns". That was our life for two years, except for the trips to Philly every three months to record Adam's progress, of which there was none.

This program was quite difficult for us. I loved my children, I loved my husband, but I needed to do this program. People were always giving to us, helping with the children, and it is not easy to be on the receiving end daily. But I believed in this program, I worked it, I was going to make this happen. We saw children get well and we met wonderful people. The program made sense and I do believe that God sent us there. It just did not work for Adam. He did not improve. His stiff little body remained stiff. His blinds eyes did not see. He could not walk, talk, smile, or eat on his own. He continued to seizure daily. What God did use the program for was to give us an opportunity to share our faith in the God we continued to love and trust. Penny and Sharon came to be a part of the Fenske family during this time. Penny was a registered nurse and Sharon was in the medical field as well. Penny traveled with us to Philadelphia to learn how she could best help Adam. She devoted many hours to patterning Adam. One Christmas 1980 she sent Adam a card with the following message:

"Dear Adam, One day I am confident you will read this yourself, but for now your mom and dad will read it to you. It's a story about how a profoundly brain-injured boy touched and changed my life. It is a story of meaning and purpose: ours together. Once upon a time in the land called Brookfield there lived a little boy named ADAM MARK FENSKE (that's you!) And although you could not speak you communicated with more hearts than the most scholarly man living in your land.

Though you could not see you provoked the greatest visions. Though you could barely move unless carried about, you moved more hearts, minds, and wills than all your able bodied friends put together. Your hearing is excellent: in fact, you hear more secrets, heartaches, and joys than anyone else does in your land. Even if you could have spoken I know that you never would share with others what in secret your friends told you. Because, Adam, you are above all else a very sensitive, loving, trusting little boy. Have you ever heard the phrase, "This is the place for opportunity?" Well, it is a phrase adults use to describe a situation or interaction that could bring into their lives something good. To me, Adam, you are a place rich with opportunity. Because of who you are I have received goodness and richness. You are softness and love in a heart prone to hardness. You are faith in the God who is faithful. You are selflessness to a soul that is selfish. You are patience and tolerance to one who is neither. Your life allows me to bring hope to hopeless hearts. You are boldness to my soul, which is fearful and timid. You are feet for me intellectual understanding of commitment. Adam, you are a place of belonging-a person and a family to love. You are healing to my hurting soul. You are the opportunity to be a part of a process that is bigger than I am. God, with you as His chosen instrument, is perfecting me. You are evidence of God's grace and redemption. Adam, you are a student at the Institutes of Human Potential, but we both have the privilege to be students at God's institute for the achievement of Christ given potential. Thank you, Adam, for the privilege of serving you and your lovely family, as a result I am changed. For who you are, Adam, I thank you. For who you are becoming, we thank

God. As a result we are changing. My present is love to you, dear Adam. Love because Christ who is love understands what it is like being helpless and dependant. He came as a baby and gave His life so that others could experience renewed life. Adam, you as His instrument, provides opportunities for renewal. You, Adam, are a heavenly agent for that living Christ God.

With love,

Penny 12–80"

This was the caliber of the people we were privileged to call friends! Sharon not only donated her time to patterning but taught Rachel, Tim, and Ben to play the piano. The children prayed for a piano, then for a teacher. God provided both. Sharon and Penny took Rachel, Ben, and Tim on a camping trip to Wisconsin Dells. They enjoyed Noah's Ark and all of the fun things families do while Gary and I couldn't go anywhere. The "program" was our life. God knew that the other children needed to be children, so He provided people like Penny and Sharon for them as well. Ben really wanted to play soccer. Needless to say, I couldn't do all the running to practice and games. God provided a woman I had never met to call and offer to drive Ben along with her son, Shawn, to soccer. Kim was another of our patterners. She was 13 years old. She wrote this letter: Dear Adam, I was thinking really hard on what to get you for Christmas. But when Lois called and asked me to do something for the booklet, I was really happy. I have had so much fun working with you and I feel really good when I come every week. I always look forward to seeing you for you are very special to me. I told a lot of people about you especially at God Squad. I am always praying for you. One day we decided to walk to your house. It was cold and raining but me and Julie both knew it was worth the walk. Julie has told me she was so happy to come and help you. She really enjoys you and the whole family and so do I. Adam, have a merry Christmas. Love, Kim Rossa. Veronica was on staff with Campus Crusade for Christ so she came when she could. She wrote, "Sometime I long for the time when you will be able to talk to me. I can see the blessing you are in so many lives to so many different people. We all just love to come and see you every week. I think about how God is making you into his masterpiece. Adam, you are one of a kind and very special to God. He plans to use your life to bring honor and glory to himself. The Lord has a wonderful plan for your life and I'm so privileged to have the opportunity to know you. It's so special to see how your mother and father love you so much and the time they want to invest into your life. You are a special blessing to all who know you. Love, Veronica" Lois helped with Adam's care twice a week. Her two daughters also helped whenever they could. Her letter really moved me. "Dear Adam, what a busy year 1980 has been. So many things Have happened to you. Last winter you went to school and He was there...Spring came and you could sit outside in the grass. Remember how the grass tickled your feet?...and He was there...Cocoa grew from a little puppy into a big dog this year...and He was there. How you loved the little bites of cookies, "doughnies" and cheesecakes that touched you tongue...and He was there...so many people with smiling faces and loving hearts came to be with you, touching you gently, moving your arms and legs so that you could learn how it feels to crawl...and He was there...the smiling people talked to you, sang to you and loved you. How good it must have felt to have the smiling people come. You much have liked them because you shared new sounds with them and worked very hard making the smiling people smile even more because of what you did...and He was there...Dear Adam, how much you must love your Mother and Father. Sometimes when you cry (and we all do that sometimes), a word from one of them quiets your tears as you stop to listen...and He was there...remember the light box, dear Adam?(Perhaps you'd like to forget it) How bright and warm the lights are, bringing healing...and He was there...You had a ride in an airplane this year. The plane took you far away to visit doctors and other people who care about you...and He was there...at home again, your basement turned into a busy place with more smiling faces coming and going, doors opening and closing, new equipment, new experiences, more loving hands...and He was there...did you like listening to Tim and Rachel play the piano? They have to work hard to learn too...and He was there. Your special slide is new this year, dear Adam .How exciting it is to watch you move yourself down the slide into the arms of a friend who is waiting to catch you at the bottom. You have learned to MOVE...all by yourself...and He was there...were you outside when Ben hunted worms in the driveway with a flashlight?...and He was there...so many thing have happened this year, dear Adam- important thing, everyday things, times of happiness and sadness...and through it all in events both big and small, God was there...caring for you in a special way...loving you...working His miracles in and through you. You are very special! You are very dear...Adam! Thank you for touching my life, with love, Lois.

My Uncle Tom had heard of our attempts to get Adam to Philadelphia. As the time came close for us to drive out there for our initial consultation, we received plane tickets for the three of us and $500.00 for expenses from my uncle. What an answer to prayer that was! It was difficult for Adam to ride in the car for long periods of time and this enabled Gary to be away from his job and us the other children for a shorter period. We flew home through Toronto to spend time with Uncle Tom. That time gave us an opportunity to share our experience of God working in our lives, of God using him to get us to Philly. I pray that God used that time and subsequent letters to soften his heart towards God. I pray that when my special Uncle Tom passed away that he had accepted God's love and forgiveness and is in Heaven today.

I also met my friend, Mary Jane. The impact she had on my life is far too great to explain. She helped pattern Adam from day one until the last day. She took over for me on Thursday afternoons and I would use her car to grocery shop. Oftentimes she paid for our groceries! She loved Adam, me, Gary, our other children, even our dog, unconditionally. On the days that I would lock myself in my bedroom, refusing to come out, unable to function, she was there. When I told her that I had nothing more to give to my husband, she was there praying. Never did she remind me that she was a deacon's wife or that she had leukemia. In those days her shining light was my Bible. When she died a couple of years later on July 5th, I cried for the world's loss of a very special woman. She truly believed "for me to live is Christ, to die is gain." I'm sure she has lots of jewels in her crown, too!

Every trip to Philadelphia was a new experience. Adam was tested, we were instructed, and at the end of two years, we knew it was time to quit. We had done our best and it was time to end one chapter and begin a new one.

Tim, Rachel, and Ben needed us as well. Gary's and my marriage had suffered tremendously.I chose to do what had been my pattern . I ran the other way. I ran away from god. I ran away from my husband, my children, my responsibilities, into the arms of my childhood sweetheart. I broke the heart of all who mattered including myself and my god .I found solace in this man whenever I would tear myself away from my crushing responsibilities and finally came clean with my husband. We separated after a month of my adulterous relationship. I didn't care. I just cared that I had a place to go where I didn't have pain, responsibility and anquish. I didn't have to look at a grossly braindamaged child, a stepchild who was acting out and hated me, two young children whom I adored and I didn't have time for and a husband that I couldn't please. The problem was I still belonged to God and He only let me go so long before He pulled me lovingly back in and I repented. Gary did forgive me as did my children and most importantly my God. We reconciled and Hannah Louise was born in August of 1983. Adam was seven, Ben was nine, and Rachel was eleven. Tim was fourteen and no longer living with us. The stress and pain of letting him go only added to the unbearable hurts we had endured. "Where was God during this time?" Of course He was there but His position in our lives was not where it should have been. God is the center—He keeps everything in perspective. He desires good for His children, but children are not always obedient. We were not that at that point in our lives.

We had moved to a new home and community during my pregnancy with Hannah. That meant a new church and the decision to home school Rachel and Ben. On the outside we were a "neat Christian family." People looked at us as special because of Adam. Many times I wanted to scream, "I didn't choose this, I'm not so great! I'm barely hanging on!" No one wanted to hear that, though, so I just smiled and did my best not to fall apart in public. I know that I became a new creature in Christ at age 15 when I prayed at a Young Life camp in Colorado. I asked the God of the universe to be my personal savior, to once and for all forgive me of my past, present, and future sins. I know that it was not possible to loose my salvation, but I was not relinquishing my pain and self-centerdness to God. Subsequently I was unhappy and blamed others instead of myself. We were still involved at church, went to a couple's Bible study in our neighborhood, had lots of great friends, but something had vanished. We had put ourselves first, not God.

Gary got a promotion during this time and was spending more time away from the home. This was increasingly burdensome for me. Adam was in "school" all day. A bus picked him up every morning and brought him home every afternoon. I hated putting him on that bus. He was absolutely helpless and alone during that hour ride. I had no idea what happened to him all day. He could not communicate in any. Did they yell at him, ignore him, show him love? I also felt guilt over sending him away. I also worried about the future. Would I be doing this until he was fifty? I was scared. I was involved in Rachel and Ben's schooling, transporting them to horseback riding lessons, soccer, baseball, and Awana. On Fridays we spent the morning at a local senior home as part of our school cirriculum. When Adam was home with us, he went everywhere we did in his little blue denim wheelchair.

The following August Rachel was 12, Ben was nine, Hannah was one, and Adam was eight. Rachel and Ben were flourishing at home and Hannah adored her big brothers and sister. She hugged and kissed Adam constantly. Her name for him was Baby. He went back to school in the fall, again on the little yellow bus. It was a long ride for him and a long day. I began to get phone calls from his speech therapist at school stating that Adam wasn't eating his lunch. I was concerned but he did seem to be putting on weight, in fact, he was getting a little chubby! How could that be, we wondered? I questioned his bus driver and he embarrassingly admitted that he was giving Adam Hardee's cinnamon rolls! The driver told us that after he picked Adam up he went to Hardee's drive thru for himself but when Adam started smacking his lips, he started sharing a roll with him every morning! School was not pleased but we were thrilled to know that Adam had a little bit of "normalcy" in his severely abnormal world. Especially when this little boy was expected to be on a food tube his entire life! We were encouraged. Maybe the healing would just be slow.

When circumstances like this would arise, I would just remind myself that God was truly in control of Adam's life. I still believed that God was going to physically heal him. Why would He have brought him this far only to let him die?

We had many well-meaning friends who also believed in the physical healing power of God. I did and still do. I am grateful to

God that He gave me a mind that doesn't question even when God says no; because it was not God's will that Adam receive healing. Almost every week people would come over to pray over Adam or to take him to a healing service that was being held somewhere in the Milwaukee area. This was not something my husband approved of, but he worked a lot of evenings so off the kids and I would go!

One night after a particularly moving service, my precious Ben waited up all night for Adam to "wake up!" Gary's disapproval came from the bitter disappointment in the children's faces when Adam didn't wake up. I truly believed that one of these services would succeed in healing Adam.

Our friend, Dave Anderson, invented a board with an alarm attached for Adam to sleep on. If Adam ever "woke up" and lifted his head, which he was unable to do, the alarm would sound. We were ready and waiting!

In the fall of 1984, I responded to a knock at our door. It was a gentleman who identified himself as a local disc jockey at the new Christian radio station in Milwaukee. He told me that he had heard about Adam (churches all over the country had heard about Adam and had sent their prayers, even Christian radio stations were praying for him) and believed that God had not healed him because of something demonic in our home—possibly secular record albums. I told him I had the complete Beatle collection, my favorite group (I was a child of the sixties!). He then told me if I gave them to him to destroy, God would surely forgive me my idol worship and heal my son! I couldn't retrieve them fast enough! We loaded all of them into the trunk of his car and off he went! I was certain that now my son would be well and the entire world would believe in Jesus when they saw a profoundly retarded child get up and walk. My father would fall onto his knees in repentance, our unsaved friends and acquaintances would flock to church, we would be reunited with Tim, and Gary and I would live happily ever after. We would watch Adam walk, talk, swim, play sports, and play the piano with his siblings. None of this was to be. Releasing the cherished albums did not heal Adam and Gary was furious with me! I needed only to trust God with Adam and quit the frenetic grasping at straws. I had so far to go and so much to learn…I worked on letting go…

Tranquility described our home after that. Our routine was becoming "normal" for us after six years with the "new Adam". We all seemed to finally accept that the old Adam was gone forever. We hired some help for Adam after school. Gary was enjoying his new responsibilities at work. Rachel and Ben continued to study at home and were best friends. Hannah adored them and they loved her to death!

Christmas was especially nice in 1984. We spent quality time with my mom and her new husband. We traveled to see my dad and visited Gary's mom. Adam was quite content to sit in his chair or on the couch where Hannah could crawl all over him. Rachel was growing into a gorgeous preteen and Ben was developing into the family "thinker". It was pleasant to have Adam home days and with the help of Diane, Linda, and Peggy, I was coping.

Gary's birthday was in January and for the first time in years, I was able to plan a dinner out for us. Peggy came and stayed with Adam while we went out to celebrate. When we got home that evening, Peggy reported that Adam was coming down with a cold, and by Saturday I was also sick in bed. Sunday was another sick day although we were sure that Adam would be well enough to go to school on Monday.

Our days began at 6 am during the week in order to get Adam up, bathed, and fed before the bus came. Gary had agreed to be that person because I was so run down. At 6:15 am I awoke to Gary's screams, "Allison, Adam's dead, Adam's dead, come quickly!" I dashed down the hallway to find Gary crying over Adam's already cold body. He was giving him CPR between his tears and pleading with God. I touched his cold stiff leg and fell to my knees. The first words from my mouth were "the Lord gives, the Lord takes away, blessed be the name of the Lord." I had remembered that Stuart Briscoe had said that when his mother died shortly before Adam. How did I feel? I don't think I did.

"Gary, Adam is gone," I said. He continued to give him CPR, crying, "No, Adam, no!" Rachel ran to call 911 and Ben stood speechless with tears streaming down his face.

Our precious, darling son—Gary called his boys "bone of my bone, flesh of my flesh", had left his crippled, helpless body at the age of 8 ½ years to walk or maybe run through the gates of Heaven into the arms of his Heavenly father.

A part of me also died that day. There is a saying that parents aren't supposed to bury their children. I certainly agree but that isn't life and that obviously isn't always the will of God. To this day I miss my little guy but would I take him back out of his mansion in Heaven where he is whole and there are no tears? Never! God had a plan for Adam's life and God makes no mistakes! Did God take him because I loved him so much? Of course not! Psalms 139 says, "you (Adam) are fearfully and wonderfully made." God knew Adam in the womb, and His plan was fulfilled for Adam in his 8-½ years in our family. Halleluiah that we have that hope and peace! The Bible, God's word to us mortals, promises us that.

The day of Adam's funeral, January 30, 1985, was blizzardly. Our dear friend and pastor, Mike Frans, performed Adam's memorial service at Elmbrook Church. It was a beautiful celebration of Adam's life and all of the hundreds of people who Adam touched were there. God had used Adam in so many people's lives. People learned to love unconditionally because of Adam. People understood that Adam in his two year old mind knew the God who made the moon, and trees, and man.

I recently asked my children to express to me how Adam's life and death has effected their lives. Rachel's letter expresses how much Adam taught her about love. She writes:

"My thoughts and feelings are hard to put into words on how my precious brother, Adam, has affected my life but I will try. Recently I realized that my only memories I have of Adam are after his brain damage. This was sad for me to realize, but true.

With this said, I will begin my thoughts…My role as the oldest child in our family took on greater meaning after Adam was brain damaged. I took on the responsibilities of one of Adam's caregivers. Mom could not do it all on her own and I took much joy in holding Adam, talking to Adam, showing him love just like I did with my other brother, Ben. I did not feel any differently about Adam and his handicaps; I still loved him for who he was, my baby brother. Whatever Mom needed, I was there ready and willing to help. Adam brought me so much joy. At times he was uncomfortable and would cry. All I had to do was go over and pick him up and hold him and he would stop. The thing that made this occurrence bring me joy was that Adam didn't do this for just anyone. He knew my voice and I could comfort him when other people couldn't. I had a connection with Adam and that never changed. Adam may not have teased me, played with me, shared secrets with me, or any other normal things brothers and sisters share, but we still shared love and time together. Thinking back on our family life as now a wife and mother made me aware of the difficult, unusual, straining, stressful situations we faced as a family together, but I never once thought that we were any different than most families growing up. I am a stronger, more passionate, driven person because of my brother. I face life head on and am willing to be challenged and challenge others. I may have grown up and matured faster than most, but I would not change much of my life for anything. I miss Adam deeply still today and I do wonder what life would be like sharing it with another brother. Adam was a special guy who taught me how to show others love unconditionally, expect the unexpected, to be willing to deal with whatever life asks of me and to continually look to my eternal resting place with anticipation. I can't wait to see Adam in Heaven and see what God has made him into."

God used Adam to forever change me. Adam taught a strong willed young mom that her children are on loan from God. My responsibility before God is to raise them up to take on that faith and responsibility with their own children one day. For many years Satan had me convinced that I failed every test given to me. This is a lie from the pit of hell. If I commit my life and my children to the Lord, all I need to do is "trust and obey, for there's no other way, to be happy in Jesus than to trust and obey."

One week after Adam died, my family was invited to a special party at Adam's school. When we pulled up at the school sweet little 19 month old Hannah started squealing, "Baby! Baby!" The darling little sister thought that that is where her "Baby" had been all week! She couldn't wait to run down the halls to Adam's classroom to see him again. Teachers and family alike stood and waited with tears running down our faces. Hannah ran from room to room looking for her beloved "Baby". How do you comfort a baby? I didn't know how but somehow we made it. The teachers had been so touched by the funeral that they had purchased a music box that played "Jesus Loves Me", the song that Laura Snyder had sung at the memorial service. God had touched their lives as well.

The letter I received from my son Ben truly reveals how much Adam touched his life. He writes:

"Mom,

I've thought a lot over the last few days about his [Adam's] impact of my life. I really haven't come up with anything earth shattering. Through that experience I learned that even the best things in life are fleeting. One must not take for granted the health of his children. After my third child passed the age of two, I was utterly relieved and thankful to have healthy children. What a blessing. I also know that flexibility and self-sacrifice is not a struggle for me, simple a way of life that I came to know and accept at a very early age.

Probably the emotion that fills me most when I think of Adam is sadness. Rarely a month goes by that my eyes don't fill up with tears as I reflect on the brother that I never got to know. I guess my self-pity and sorrow fail to allow me to appreciate the tremendous good that Adam did for so many. I trust that Adam touched those people in a unique and positive way, yet I still am sorry that he wasn't there for me and the rest of us.

I must say that I did learn a great deal about love through him; the years of toil and sacrifice that our family and the volunteers went through to help him, the way that Hannah adored him, and the haunting screams from Dad when he learned that his beloved son had died. Adam didn't know what love was, he made our lives extremely difficult, but one doesn't need to give love or deserve love, he simple gets it from those who love him unconditionally."

Last summer was Adam's 27th birthday. I still go to his grave. I still miss him and long for the day when I will see him face to face. Often I will whisper a prayer of thanksgiving that Adam is "up there with you, God." Gary's and my marriage did not survive our ordeal. We separated six months after Adam's death. We had pain and unresolved anger that just plain hurt too much. I did fail that test with many regrets and sorrow. When Gary and I separated, I had a major decision to make. I needed to make my faith my own. He had not only been the head of our home, but also directed my spiritual life. I don't say this to criticize but to state a fact. Other than accepting Jesus as my Savior personally, he controlled the rest. I hypothetically went along for the ride. He volunteered our help at children's church, Bible study, Bible clubs for the children, and encouraged my growth as a Christian. When he left, my faith faltered for a long time. I stepped out of God's will and went my own way for longer than I am willing to admit. But praise the Lord for His steadfast love and everlasting mercy. He lifted me up out of the pit and helped me to repent and again run into His tender arms of love. As I taught my children many years ago, "God will never leave Allison!" Nine years ago, I remarried. Patrick and I began our journey together and with God. It has been bumpy at times but we continue to grow and love each other. Pat has encouraged and blessed my life. Halleluia! My faith is now my own!

The letter I received from my youngest, Hannah, is different from the rest, since she wasn't around for most of Adam's short life. She writes:

"To say how Adam has affected my life is a tough one because I don't remember him at all. I think it's had a great affect on how I was raised though. You told me once that you think you and Gary would still be married today. Perhaps I would have grown up with a dad, which would make me a vastly different person. I honestly have no idea how I would be. I would probably be much more shy and less like you! I don't know if I would be married because much of my pursuit of marriage is because of my need for that male love and attention. Don't get me wrong, I don't feel like my life has been cheated of any relationship, because it hasn't. Not having a constant father figure has obviously been a challenge, but I think I've been immensely blessed through you and our special relationship. If Adam were alive, I would probably not be as much of your baby, especially if he was still brain damaged today. I might feel ignored or jealous. Maybe I wouldn't have been born at all...I now think, after reading your book, that I would know you much less of a person. It sounded to me like before Adam's death and your divorce, you were a lot more busy, more focused on doing things, activities, and everything. Not that that is bad, but when I was growing up, it was more about spending time with me, having me involved in things, you were always there whenever I needed you. I'm not sure if you would have opened up to me as much as a person, maybe I would just be your child, and not your friend. I don't know...it's hard because I didn't know you then. You just seem to be a different person now, a better person. I did want to tell you how proud I am of you writing this book. I'm so excited that you did something you've always wanted to do. A lot of people never get to that point. I think you are one of the strongest, most loving people I have ever met. I'm not just saying this as your daughter but as a woman who has observed you throughout the past twenty years. In a way, I am glad it was only you and me for such a long time...Because God has used Adam and you to touch a lot of lives-including mine."

Rachel is 31 now and mother of three-Luke, Adam and Chloe. Ben is 29 and father to Jacob, Courtney, and Alex. Hannah is newly married to Christopher and again a new chapter in my life begins. May I always honor the name of God! Forever I will be blessed that God gave me the privilege to be a mom to Tim, Rachel, Ben, Adam, and Hannah. God continues to use the memory of Adam as I relate to my grandchildren. My passion is to show them "Jesus in Grandma." I remind them that their Uncle Adam loved God and that he is alive and in Heaven with God where we will all be someday. How exciting!

Adam was ready to enter the gates of Heaven when he died on January 28, 1985. Jill Briscoe once said, "Just be sure that when it's your time to die, that you are ready." If you have honored my son by reading this short story of a very meaningful life, I pray that you, too, are ready when your time is up on earth and that you can run into the arms of your heavenly father as my son did.

0-595-31313-2

Printed in the United States
38168LVS00003B/125